IMAGES
of America

YOSEMITE
NATIONAL PARK
AND VICINITY

This Carleton E. Watkins photograph of Yosemite Falls shows both the waterfall and the handmade matte that Watkins used for his display. Watkins was the first to extensively photograph Yosemite from the valley to the Mariposa Grove of Big Trees using a mammoth glass-plate camera, with glass negatives measuring nearly two square feet. Each negative had to be hand coated with photographic emulsion, exposed while wet, hand-processed, dried, and then returned to San Francisco where contact prints were made. This photograph can now be found in the Wawona Hotel.

ON THE COVER: Wawona General Store is pictured during the Washburn years (see page 64). (Courtesy Al Gordon.)

IMAGES
of America

YOSEMITE
NATIONAL PARK
AND VICINITY

Leroy Radanovich

ARCADIA
PUBLISHING

Published by Arcadia Publishing
Charleston SC, Chicago IL, Portsmouth NH, San Francisco CA

Printed in the United States of America

Library of Congress Catalog Card Number: 2006922942

For all general information contact Arcadia Publishing at:
Telephone 843-853-2070
Fax 843-853-0044
E-mail sales@arcadiapublishing.com
For customer service and orders:
Toll-Free 1-888-313-2665

Visit us on the Internet at www.arcadiapublishing.com

CONTENTS

ACKNOWLEDGMENTS

Many people made outstanding contributions to this volume on Yosemite's history. For the section on Fish Camp, I wish to thank old friends Bob and Lynn Keller. Longtime Fish Camp residents, the late Niles and June Millar, also contributed heavily to this section and the community of Fish Camp mourns her passing.

Roger McElligott and Glen Power of Mariposa both provided significant collections of photographs, as did Keith Walklet of Yosemite Park and Curry Company. Delaware North and Becky Chambers of the decorating firm Chambers Lorenz gave me the opportunity to research the photographs in the Yosemite Museum Library.

The inherited photograph albums of Stan Hollingsworth and the collection of Sid Ledson (courtesy of Ed Hardy) both added many excellent photographs. My brother-in-law John Cadrette allowed me to use photographs of Hetch Hetchy from his family collection. These photographs date from a time when John's father, Roy Earl Cadrette, worked as a cowboy in Hetch Hetchy Valley, Yosemite Valley's late, great twin.

I also wish to recognize the contribution of Hank Johnson's publication, *Thunder in the Mountains*, for reinforcing my knowledge of early logging efforts in the Sugar Pine area.

Thanks to you all for these fine contributions.

INTRODUCTION

The part of the Sierra Nevada encompassing the Yosemite region became the earliest of the ranges to be discovered for its economic potential. Soon after its discovery, Yosemite Valley's incredible beauty stimulated the building of hotels and way stations for visitors from around the world. Notables such as Galen Clark, photographer Carleton E. Watkins, Jessie Benton Fremont, and Sen. John Conness of California played critical roles in getting the State of California to designate Yosemite Valley and the Mariposa Grove of Big Trees as a park. The balance of the area around the valley, however, did not receive full protection until the efforts of John Muir resulted in the creation of Yosemite National Park in 1890.

The earliest use of the area in and around Yosemite Valley was for livestock grazing. Small ranchers from the foothills brought sheep and cattle to the summer meadows, which provided the green feed that many coming from the Eastern and Midwestern states were used to. The long dry periods in the foothills were not easy to cope with, and in many cases, the quality of the livestock suffered. At first, most livestock raised in California (especially cattle) were for the purpose of hides and tallow so poor-quality pastures were of little consequence.

From the 1850s to modern times, the mountain industries responded to a growing demand for lumber in the newly settled state, particularly by the many gold mines that were being developed. Frequent fires, especially in San Francisco, required that rebuilding materials be prepared and shipped to the cities. While much of the lumber for San Francisco came by ship from the north coast and from the east, many gold rush towns had frequent fires, which necessitated instant repairs and rebuilding. For example, the town of Mariposa lost 63 structures—most of its commercial area—in 1966. Aside from lumber, brick, adobe, and steel were also in demand.
Harvesting the Sierra's redwoods for structural lumber proved a disaster as the fiber in the wood was very short and thus provided little strength. Many of the trees harvested from the Fresno Grove and others were split into grape stakes.

The once-primitive wilderness, formerly inhabited only by Native Americans with simple needs, was now growing and developing. A sawmill, set up in Yosemite Valley by James Mason Hutchings, became the employment place of John Muir. The rapid growth of lumber technology denuded the forests south of Yosemite as many millions of board feet were cut to meet demand.

As wealth accumulated in California, the need for some form of recreation in the Yosemite region arose. James Mason Hutchings promoted the first hotel in Yosemite Valley in his *California* magazine, and soon others were developing resorts both inside and outside Yosemite Valley. Galen Clark came to Wawona (then Palachum) in 1856, built a cabin, and soon found his lodging and meals in demand. To the south of Wawona, a number of resorts developed in turn, thus starting the recreation industry known today.

As the gold rush waned, searching further into the mountains and east across the Sierras for more mineral development resulted in the Tioga Road, a number of small mining camps, and the town of Bodie. Today modern highways traverse the area where wagons and pack mules once traveled. By 1994, almost four million visitors a year came to Yosemite, and perhaps a million more recreated in the Sierra surrounding the park.

This book, designed through the photographs that endure, gives some indication of the rapid development, destruction, and enduring use that characterizes the Sierra around Yosemite. The people who worked and lived here were independent, tough, brawling, and proud. They tamed to some degree, the wildest environment in the West.

Upper and Lower Yosemite Falls, along with the Merced River, make as lovely a view today as they did hundreds of years past.

One

CARLETON E. WATKINS AND EARLY PHOTOGRAPHERS

Carleton Emmons Watkins came to California with Collis P. Huntington (later to become an industrial baron) from Oneona, New York, in 1849. Huntington planned to open a hardware store in Sacramento, and Watkins was to work for him. Floods and fire in the hardware store ended Watkins career as a clerk, however, and he moved to San Francisco, where he went to work in the Daguerreotype photographic studio of Robert Vance. Working for Vance advanced Watkins's knowledge of photographic arts, especially in learning the new technology of negative/positive photography. This large-scale format opened the way for dramatic photographs of landscapes and architectural subjects and, by 1860, Watkins traveled to Mariposa to make mammoth glass-plate photographs of the various assets of the Fremont Grant (probably the first opportunity for photography to be used in a commercial sense). A chance visit to Yosemite Valley with Treanor Park, late in 1860, introduced Watkins to this special place.

By 1861, Watkins was ensconced in Yosemite, making glass-plate and stereo views of the magnificent valley and high country. In 1866, he had photographed Yosemite for the J. D. Whitney Survey and had begun copyrighting his stereo work. From Watkins's early 1861 work, President Lincoln and Congress gained knowledge of Yosemite and granted the valley and the Mariposa Grove of Big Trees to the State of California for the purpose of creating a park.

Watkins continued to work in the west for many years, covering the spread of the railroad as the economic tie that bound California to itself and the rest of the world. By 1890, his eyesight began to fail, and during the 1906 earthquake and fire in San Francisco, his studio was destroyed along with his negatives and inventory of prints. Destitute and blind, he was eventually committed to Napa State Hospital, where he died in 1916.

He was followed by another talented photographer, Eadweard J. Muybridge, who learned the trade in his native county of England. Muybridge started photographing Yosemite in 1868, consciously choosing different perspectives than Watkins used. He last photographed in Yosemite in 1872.

Watkins became the preeminent landscape photographer of the Far West for more than 40 years, beginning in 1860. Muybridge's career was cut short by personal issues and health. Nontheless, both men opened up Yosemite for the world to see.

El Capitan has stood for eons as a silent and dramatic sentinel over Yosemite Valley. (Photograph by Carleton E. Watkins.)

Here is a dramatic photograph of Yosemite Valley taken from Old Inspiration Point. The tree in the foreground was limbed to prevent the fantastic view from being obscured. (Photograph by Carleton E. Watkins.)

This photograph of Yosemite Valley's North Dome and Washington's Column shows streaks due to an uneven coating of emulsion on the glass plate. As Watkins became more proficient at coating plates, this phenomenon ceased. (Photograph by Carleton E. Watkins.)

Yosemite Falls is seen here from across a meadow in Yosemite Valley, with stands of native trees in the foreground. (Photograph by Carleton E. Watkins.)

The two rock outcroppings in the center of this photograph are called the Cathedral Spires, seen from the floor of Yosemite Valley. (Photograph by Carleton E. Watkins.)

Here is the lovely Bridalveil Falls, a perennial favorite for visitors to Yosemite Valley. (Photograph by Carleton E. Watkins.)

Nevada Falls, pictured here, is another favorite destination above the valley. (Photograph by Carleton E. Watkins.)

Vernal Falls has long been a beloved and photogenic spot at Yosemite. (Photograph by Carleton E. Watkins.)

Cathedral Spires and Cathedral Rocks are pictured high above the Merced River in Yosemite Valley. The high cliffs around the valley are popular with climbers and photographers. (Photograph by Carleton E. Watkins.)

This view of Yosemite Valley's Cathedral Rock also shows the "Gun Sight," the deep notch between the peaks that resembles a sight on a rifle. (Photograph by Carleton E. Watkins.)

This Yosemite Valley view shows the reflection of El Capitan in Merced River. (Photograph by Carleton E. Watkins.)

Yosemite Valley is pictured from Bridalveil Meadow. (Photograph by Carleton E. Watkins.)

This view of Yosemite Valley looks west. (Photograph by Carleton E. Watkins.)

Here is another view of Yosemite Valley. (Photograph by Carleton E. Watkins.)

This photograph of Yosemite Falls is attributed to Watkins but is signed by I. W. Taber, who bought Watkins's negatives after his business failed. Soon Taber was making his own negatives. All Watkins's and Taber's negatives, in both men's possession, were destroyed in the San Francisco earthquake and fire of 1906.

The unidentified photographer of this image titled it "Yosemite Valley Early Vernal Falls." (Photographer unidentified.)

This view of Yosemite Valley shows the wide-open spaces of the valley and meadows. The area was likely kept in good shape due to the regular burning each fall by Native Americans, similar to the "controlled burns" done today by the Park Service.

18

Here is a striking photograph of Yosemite Valley's Nevada Falls and Liberty Cap. Photographer Muybridge chose to not repeat Carleton Watkins's compositional approach to Yosemite subjects, and critics praised the new approach, while at the same time calling Watkins's work "familiar." Muybridge and Watkins had somewhat of an adversarial relationship, but both are remembered today as preeminent landscape photographers. Muybridge's career was cut short by the killing of his wife's lover. Although acquitted of the crime, he ended his stay in the United States and returned to England. (Photograph by Eadweard J. Muybridge.)

Here are the lovely and photogenic Vernal Falls above Yosemite Valley. Once again, Muybridge chose a typically romantic perspective for this view. (Photograph by Eadweard Muybridge.)

Yosemite Falls empties into the lovely and rocky Merced River in this stirring photograph. (Photograph by Eadweard Muybridge.)

Yosemite Valley's Tenaya Canyon and Half Dome are captured here in this stunning photograph called "The Domes." With this view, Muybridge captured a more romantic and less classical view of the valley than many of his contemporaries. (Photograph by Eadweard Muybridge.)

Here is a portion of the vast and seldom-photographed Yosemite backcountry. Though it has many lovely attributes, the difficulty of getting to the park's more primitive high-country areas has meant that for many years, photographers and visitors alike have preferred the scenic and easy access of Yosemite Valley.

An unknown photographer took this photograph of a nearly blind Carleton E. Watkins being lead away from his burning studio and gallery on Montgomery Street in San Francisco after the earthquake of 1906. Tragically, all of his negatives and prints were destroyed, and only originals in private and public collections survive. He went to live with his daughter for a time but later was placed in the Napa State Hospital, where he died on June 23, 1916. He left a remarkable collection of photographic work, without which there would be far less knowledge about the pioneer days of the American West. Watkins is buried in an unmarked grave.

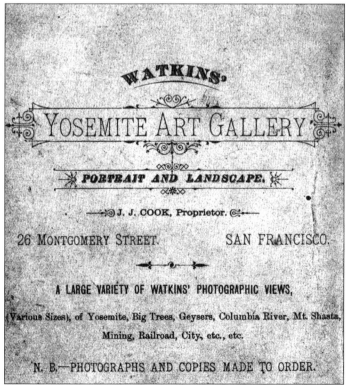

Here is the back side of a "portrait card," by Carleton E. Watkins, showing J. J. Cooke as owner of Watkins's gallery. (Photograph by Eadweard Muybridge.)

Two

YOSEMITE SOUTH

An abundance of timber and meadows has always defined the area south of Yosemite Valley. Vast stands of pine, fir, and cedar covered the Sierra, with an occasional sprinkling of giant redwoods. There to cull these vast stands was the Madera Sugar Pine Company, a very large operation that harvested and processed over a billion board feet of timber on more than 62,000 acres. The milled lumber was transported by flume 60 miles to the city of Madera for further finishing. Occasional remnants of the flume can be found, but only the foundations remain, as well as the concrete structure of the boiler room and a few cabins in the village of Sugar Pine.

From 1874 until 1931, the sounds of logging dominated the Sierra area south of Yosemite. Although oxen were used initially, steam from railroads and donkey engines provided the rugged power needed to move the timber from forest to mill. Many of the pioneer families of Mariposa, Madera, and Fresno County lived and worked at the various lumber camps and mills, the greatest being the Madera Sugar Pine Company. Today one can experience the thrill of riding the "logger" through the forest on the Yosemite Mountain Sugar Pine Railroad excursion on Highway 41, south of Fish Camp.

Albert and Annie Philp first built a store at Fish Camp, then later a lodge and cabins, and over the years many facilities have been located here. The Philps sold their timber claim to the Madera Sugar Pine Company, which constructed tracks through the town. When the lumber company ended its operations, the original 40 acres were sold Charlie and Maude Beery, who added other lodges and facilities, some of which were crushed in snowstorm around 1937.

The Beerys sold Fish Camp to Harold J. Baker, a Merced real-estate broker and investor. He subdivided Fish Camp for summer cottages, and left the property to his daughter and her husband, Evelyn R. and Robert O. Keller. Baker also built the Silver Tip Lodge, which the Keller's inherited. This lodge became a favorite stopping point for visitors to the Yosemite region but burned down in 1980. A new hotel, also named Silver Tip, will soon be added to the community. In 1990, the Tenaya Lodge opened on property bordering Fish Camp and has proven to be a welcome addition.

Moving millions of board feet of timber to the Madera Sugar Pine mill required the power of steam engines. This one, known as "Betsy," was of unknown origin but served the Madera Sugar Pine mill faithfully from 1899 until it was scrapped in 1937.

Whole families moved with their logger and sawmill-worker husbands and would often join them for social events on Sundays. The Madera Sugar Pine mill had a hospital and school for workers and their families. Looking back over the hospitals' log books today shows a whole litany of human experiences, including births, deaths, and accidents.

The backbreaking job of moving logs through the woods depended on the strength of the men and animals. These large draft animals were prized for their strength and were the unsung heroes of California's early building industry.

Using the steam donkey, or engine, these workers are organizing logs on a landing, very difficult and dirty work. The poles that the men are holding were used for rolling and moving the immense logs by hand.

Wood-fired steam donkeys, mounted on skids, provided the muscle to move heavy timber to railcars for transport to the mill. Once hooked by cable to a tree, these engines could drag themselves through the woods to the desired work site.

In this photograph, a steam donkey and more traditional "horsepower" combine to skid logs along a track, using other logs as a guide.

Moving a heavy engine along a track through wooded terrain could be challenging, as this photograph depicts. Note the controls for operation. Breaking cables could be very dangerous, especially if they whipped back towards the engine and operator. Many injuries and deaths resulted from moving equipment.

Here a Shay engine and load of logs moves through the deforested landscape on its way to the mill.

Tracks approach the mill and millpond where the logs will be off-loaded by booms over the railroad tracks.

The logs are off-loaded into the millpond before processing in the mill.

After the logs hit the millpond water, they were floated toward the sawmill, pictured in the background of this photograph, with the boiler house on the left.

A group of visitors standing in the lumber-loading area takes in this view of the mill. From here, cut lumber was bundled and clamped before being sent on its epic flume journey to Madera.

In this photograph, a survey party sets grading for the building of new tracks.

Logging camps were typically built of movable buildings, which were transferred from camp to camp on railroad flat cars.

Accidents in the woods were common, especially when heavy logs would overturn a car or when a trestle collapsed.

High lead, or "highline," logging was a technique used to move logs from the mountaintop to the landing across deep ravines. Tall trees were topped with pulleys attached to guide cables, which were strung in turn to other trees some distance away. This way, logs could be lifted from ravines and transferred over long distances to landings.

A log moves along the line toward a landing.

A log arrives at end of line, where it can be loaded for further processing.

Log trains needed circuitous routes to the mills because of the steep terrain. The railroad grades had to be gentle to allow the loaded trains to arrive safely and so as not to overload the engines. Many of the roads now used throughout the forest were originally railroad roadbeds.

Lookouts, such this one on Signal Peak, were used to spot fires that could be set inadvertently by passing steam engines in the woods.

The Shay engine, made in Lima, Ohio, was slow but very strong and was the standard engine used in travel through the woods. All wheels on the engine and tender were driven by direct drive. Today one can hop a ride on a restored Shay engine through the woods at the Yosemite Mountain Sugar Pine Railroad, just south of Fish Camp on Highway 41.

This log train is taking the timber from one tree to the mill at Sugar Pine. The massive trees in this area dwarfed the locomotives.

In this photograph, logs wait for their turn in the millpond before being processed.

These logs have seen their last days of freedom, as they move from the pond to the sawmill.

This crew's job was to keep the mill's saws sharp. It was a critical, full-time job.

Albert Philp's general merchandise store and post office served the needs of loggers, mill workers, and their families.

By 1881, Albert and Annie Philp had added the Fish Camp House. Most of their customers were loggers, though a few tourists occasionally came through.

Gradually the Fish Camp House grew as add-ons were built to accommodate the growing number of workers.

A porch and additional buildings, as well as a large two-story dormitory, dominated the scene at Fish Camp until sometime in the 1940s.

In 1926, Charlie and Maude Beery acquired Fish Camp from the Madera Sugar Pine Company and built a hotel made of unpeeled cedar logs. Unfortunately, the logs dried out rather quickly and within two years, the building burned to the ground in a matter of minutes.

The Beerys rebuilt after the fire, only to have snow from a heavy storm collapse the main structure in 1937. Gasoline pumps were added near the tall yellow pine, presaging the gas station.

The Beerys rebuilt the lodge using two young carpenters from the California Conservation Corps (CCC) camp in Wawona, thus creating Fish Camp Lodge. The large white dormitory building had been improved, and Standard Oil products were sold at the gas station.

Winter at the Fish Camp can be a snowbound experience. The store and resort cabins remained open throughout the season, however.

Here are some of the rustic cabins of Davenport's Trading Post in Fish Camp, now mostly gone.

Fish Camp, because of copious snowfall, is a favorite play area for families. People from the Yosemite region, as well as from outlying towns like Oakhurst, Coarsegold, Madera, and Fresno, are drawn to winter sports in the Sierra National Forest.

A group of investors, headed by Harold J. Baker, bought the Fish Camp property and began redevelopment. By 1944, the old lodge and dormitory were removed and the new Silver Tip Lodge built. By 1960, a four-unit lodging facility was also added.

Harold Baker left the property to his daughter Evelyn R. Keller and her husband, Robert O. Keller. At various times, the Kellers operated or leased the lodge and other facilities. For more than 40 years, they have also been active in developing subdivisions for recreational homes. In 1990, the Tenaya Lodge was built near the community, and a new Silver Tip Lodge is slated for construction in the future. The Apple Tree Inn and White Chief Mountain Lodge also offer accommodation in the community, while the Fish Camp General Store continues its tradition of serving the public.

The Beerys, along with a number of other investors, also purchased the Yosemite Mountain Ranch around the same time they bought Fish Camp. This private, 3,300-acre ranch was acquired from Madera Sugar Pine Company. During the Depression, the Beerys relinquished their interest amidst declining public development.

Fred Wass of Mariposa leads the pack train in this photograph taken at the Yosemite Trails Pack Station. Pack operations started in Fish Camp, and later at Skidder Camp on the Jackson Gate Road. This enterprise has continued serving the recreation needs of the public for more than 70 years.

This brochure cover from the Silver Tip Lodge touts a relaxed and friendly atmosphere for those visiting Fish Camp.

Three

MARIPOSA GROVE OF BIG TREES AND WAWONA

In March 1851, two companies of the Mariposa Battalion passed through the meadows of Palachum, looking for the band of Native Americans who had been raiding mining camps and stores around Mariposa County. During their search, they discovered and entered Yosemite Valley, becoming the first white men to do so.

Among the second group of visitors, led by James Mason Hutchings, was Galen Clark, a gold miner from Mariposa. In 1856, having been diagnosed with an incurable case of consumption, Clark, age 42, decided to return to the meadow that he had visited on his trip, intending on spending his last days in the mountains that he loved so much. However, his health improved and he lived 54 more years, dying a few days short of the age of 96. Clark discovered a grove of magnificent sequoia redwoods, which he called the Mariposa Grove. Aware of the destruction of sequoias in other sections of the Sierra, he was reluctant to reveal the location of the grove, but eventually saw it protected by the federal government with a grant to the State of California for creation of a park.

Clark spent the rest of his life leading the preservation efforts for both Yosemite Valley and the Mariposa Grove. During a busy life, he became a fixture in Yosemite and Wawona, serving as the guardian of Yosemite Valley, which is similar to a ranger, at least three times.

In 1874, Clark sold his property to Albert Henry Washburn for $1,000 and the cancellation of $20,000 in debt. Washburn built the Wawona Hotel, adjacent buildings, and a wagon road into Yosemite Valley. Meanwhile, the Mariposa Grove of Big Trees became a major tourist attraction.

The meadows in front of the Wawona Hotel provided pasture for a dairy herd, as well as a landing strip for early airplanes. Albert Henry Washburn and his brothers acquired the property and through three generations, became fixtures south of the park. In 1932, the Department of Interior acquired the Washburn property, adding it to Yosemite National Park and connecting it to the Mariposa Grove. Operated from that time on by the Yosemite Park and Curry Company (and currently Delaware North) as concessionaires, the elegant old hotel is a favorite of many returning visitors.

Here is Galen Clark, photographed around 1861 by Watkins in Mariposa Grove. He built his cabin in Palachum (now Wawona) and, in 1856, discovered the Mariposa Grove of giant sequoias (along with trail builder Milton Mann). Clark led a lifelong effort to preserve and protect the giant trees.

This cluster of redwood sequoias occurs at the Mariposa Grove, one of the largest such groves in California. The composition of this tree, with its short fiber base, makes it unsuitable for use in construction. When one of these trees is felled or harvested, it breaks into sections, much like a matchstick. Lumber from these trees has little structural strength.

Redwood sequoias, pictured here in winter, have high concentrations of tannin, making them fire resistant. If exposed to fire or lightning, normally only dead sections of the tree, or the very tops, would combust.

This magnificent tree, the largest tree in the Mariposa Grove, is named Grizzly Giant. While not the tallest in the world, it has become the symbol of the grove, and it is the site of many photographs with dignitaries, presidents, and paupers.

When Pres. Theodore Roosevelt visited Yosemite in 1903, he was joined by John Muir and others for this portrait in front of the Grizzly Giant.

Groups of ordinary citizens, usually guests at the Wawona Hotel, would tour the Mariposa Grove in carriages and be photographed with the Grizzly Giant.

Here is Galen Clark as he appeared in later life. Clark served as guardian of the Mariposa Grove and Yosemite Valley for the State of California.

Galen Clark built a cabin in the upper grove; the cabin pictured here is a reconstructed version. The structure still serves as a memorial to Clark and as a visitor center.

Clark, seen here with photographer Julius Boysen, visited the grove often.

Cavalry troops from the army patrolled Yosemite National Park from 1891 until 1914, when the military administration ended. Until Yosemite Valley's return to the federal government in 1906, headquarters for the army was in Wawona. Here they pose on the Fallen Monarch in Mariposa Grove.

In 1881, a tunnel was cut through the Wawona Tree and it became a favorite destination for travelers to Mariposa Grove. Here driver Eddie Gordon takes a group of tourists through the tree.

In this photograph, Pres. William Howard Taft visits the tunnel tree with Galen Clark and members of Yosemite's army regiment.

President Roosevelt and his party visit the stately Wawona Tree in this *c.* 1903 photograph.

Guide Eddie Gordon leads a party through the Mariposa Grove in this photograph. Three generations of Gordon family men served as stage drivers and guides for the Wawona Hotel.

Although the first automobile arrived in Yosemite in 1901, internal combustion engines were banned until 1913. Buses, such as this one, soon replaced horse-drawn conveyances in the Mariposa Grove.

It was always a festive occasion when large groups passed through the Wawona Tree, as seen in this photograph.

By the 1930s, the Yosemite Park and Curry Company, longtime Yosemite concessionaires, became a Cadillac dealership and purchased a number of buses such as this one. They were used until well after World War II.

The Big Tree Lodge, located in the upper grove, was built and operated by the Yosemite Park and Curry Company.

Galen Clark, seated at left on the log, watches as partners Edwin and Hulduth Moore greet visitors to Clark's ranch at Palachum (Wawona). Clark proposed to live out his days in the meadows, but he became an innkeeper and later guardian of Yosemite.

By 1875, Clark was deep in debt and sold the Palachum property to Albert Henry Washburn. In 1876, Albert and his wife, Jean Bruce Washburn, built the Wawona Hotel after fire destroyed Clark's cottage in 1878. The Washburns changed the name of Palachum to Wawona, and the property remained in the family until 1931. This 1878 photograph is the first known picture of the hotel.

Washburn carries a turkey feather duster under his arm to dust off passengers after their long trip (and before they enter his brand new hotel).

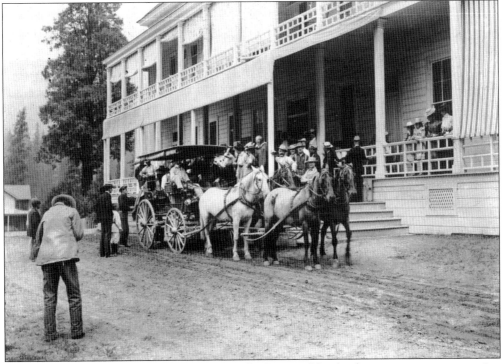

A photography session commemorates the early Wawona Hotel, where passengers are wearing dusters after the long ride. Ed Washburn is seated next to the driver.

This early photograph of the Wawona Hotel shows decorations used for special occasions. A third floor in the hotel was designated for the family, but it proved to be too hot in the summer and too cool in the winter. Mrs. Washburn set up a parlor in the south end of the hotel for the family.

Additional structures were added to the Wawona property over the years. In 1876, Clark Cottage (in the center between the trees) was built. Moore Cottage (also named Little Brown, seen behind the hotel) was added later. The small building on the right was known as Small White and occasionally used by the family.

After 1917, the Washburn family added a dining room at the north end of the hotel, as well as a large building called the annex, which had provisions for a shop on the ground floor and a sunroom for small gatherings. A swimming tank and a golf course were also added.

Water diverted from the south fork of the Merced River formed a small lake named Stella, after Estella Washburn, John Washburn's wife. The lake provided ice for the summer. This crew of ice cutters includes Mariposa man George Washington Walker, in the middle to the left of the ice block.

Under the Washburns, the Wawona Hotel operated in the spring, summer, and fall, often closing after Christmas and not opening again until April or May. The hotel was the center of a farm, and farm animals, such as hogs, often grazed the grounds in the off-season.

With the advent of the automobile, Washburn converted his stagecoaches to motor-driven buses and provided transportation to the park from a number of locations. He also installed the first telephone line to Yosemite Valley.

The Wawona Hotel, pictured here in 1990, is still a favorite resort for many Californians. Weddings are frequently held here, as well as a western barbecue on Saturday nights in the summer. (Photograph by author.)

The cavalry detachment from the Presidio in San Francisco poses in this Wawona-area photograph.

The cavalry unit from the Presidio in San Francisco patrolled Yosemite National Park from the late 1890s. They were stationed at Wawona, just inside the park boundary. This photograph was taken in Mariposa Grove at Grizzly Giant Tree

Camp Hoyle was a concessionaire setup just inside the park on the site of the old cavalry camp at Wawona.

A baseball team representing the Wawona Hotel played other teams from areas such as Sugar Pine and Fish Camp. Many of the players worked at the hotel, but some were employed as packers and lumbermen.

The Washburns also built a general store, a dance pavilion, tennis courts, and the low-cost Sequoia Hotel. All burned down at various times, except the tennis courts.

Many families from Mariposa and other lower areas summered in the cool air of Wawona. At left is Fred Schlageter, summer postmaster and carpenter, with members of the McElliogtt, Farnsworth, and Thorne families from Mariposa.

Johnnie Bruce was a brother-in-law to Albert Henry Washburn. He established a homestead in Section Number 35, which, because the homestead predated the park, is today private land within Yosemite National Park.

Jay Cook Bruce, Albert Bruce's son, became a state hunter noted for his ability to track and kill cougars that were a threat to mountain communities.

Four

GLACIER POINT AND THE HIGH COUNTRY

Nowhere on the rim of Yosemite Valley offers such an incredible view as Glacier Point. Dominating the scene to the east is Half Dome, with Tenaya Canyon to the left and Clark Range and Little Yosemite Valley to the right. In the distance are the Cathedral Range and the high country of Yosemite National Park. Today this is one of the most visited points in Yosemite for visitors seeking its panorama of the valley and Yosemite Falls across the canyon. Just to the west of Glacier Point is Sentinel Dome, another dramatic feature of the high country.

As early as the 1870s, Glacier Point attracted visitors who had to climb the cliffs to reach the point. James McCauley built the Four Mile Trail in order to access the spot where he planned to build a hotel. His Mountain House became the destination for many who would ride horses and mules and hike the steep four miles to visit the overlook. In 1903, Pres. Theodore Roosevelt visited with John Muir at Glacier Point, thereby establishing the return of Yosemite Valley to the federal government.

By 1918, a road was built extending from the Wawona Road to Glacier Point, and the Park Service contracted a first class hotel to be built at the point. The resulting facilities were beautiful but were destroyed by fire in 1969, never to be replaced. Glacier Point today is a day-use area, and the Four Mile Trail is still the favorite route for many hearty souls.

Poor visitation to the park during the early days of the Depression was a problem for both the Park Service and the Curry Company. The opening of State Route 140, or the "All Year Highway," through Mariposa in 1926 offered more opportunity for year-round use. Working with the Park Service, the Curry Company started a winter program along the Glacier Point Road, an arrangement that led to the opening of Badger Pass Ski Resort in 1935. This required the Park Service to keep the Glacier Point Road open as far as Badger, which subsequently evolved into one of the best intermediate ski areas in the country. Cross-country trekking was soon added to the delightful activities originating from this resort.

Glacier Point juts out 3,000 feet over Yosemite Valley. The panorama from this point affords views to El Capitan in the west, Yosemite Falls in the north to Tenaya Canyon, and Half Dome and Cathedral Range to the east. Vernal and Nevada Falls and Little Yosemite are to the southeast, and the Clark Range is beyond those. (Photograph by Carleton E. Watkins.)

This view encompasses Glacier Point to the east and southeast, with Half Dome, Vernal and Nevada Falls, and Little Yosemite Valley dominating the foreground.

Taken from the west end of the valley, this photograph shows Sentinel Dome, Glacier Point, and Half Dome in the haze to the east. This vantage point from the Mariposa-Wawona Road near Fort Monroe was the southern entrance to the valley until 1935. Bridalveil Fall and Cathedral Rocks dominate the foreground.

Photographer George Fiske liked to photograph various items perched on Glacier Point's jutting rock outcrops. In this view, his donkey is posed for a postcard. It was not recorded how he got the donkey to assume the required position, but he was obviously a marvelous photographer. (Photograph by George Fiske.)

For this photograph, Fiske photographed Kitty Tatsch and a friend, maids at the Sentinel Hotel in Yosemite Valley. This scene has since become one of the most famous from Yosemite. (Photograph by George Fiske.)

In 1900, Oliver Lippincott came to Yosemite in the first automobile to enter the park. Somehow his 1900 Locomobile traversed over the 1882 wagon road built by John Conway—all the way to Glacier Point via Wawona. By 1907, automobiles were banned from the park, but were allowed in again by 1913.

In 1903, Pres. Theodore Roosevelt was photographed on Glacier Point with John Muir. The purpose of the trip was to discuss the return of the Yosemite Valley and Mariposa Grove grants to the federal government from the State of California for inclusion in Yosemite National Park, which had been formed in 1890.

It is 3.000 feet to the Bottom
And no undertaker to meet you
TAKE NO CHANCES.
There is a difference
Between bravery and just plain
ORDINARY FOOLISHNESS.

Before the construction of a metal railing at Glacier Point by the Park Service, a simple warning sign was thought to be sufficient.

Washburn Point was established on Glacier Point Road, giving the visitors a clear view of Vernal (lower) and Nevada (upper) falls, as well as the Valley of the Little Yosemite.

By 1875, George Anderson made the first ascent of Half Dome from the east side. He installed cables, making the climb and descent easier. Each year, cables in the formation are removed in the fall and reinstalled in the spring. Climbing the face of Half Dome was first accomplished in 1958. (Photograph by author.)

With Nevada Falls in the background, this group of riders heads for Glacier Point via the Panorama Trail.

After completion of the Four Mile Trail by John Conway in 1872, James McCauley built the first hotel at Glacier Point, named the Mountain House, in 1876.

The 1882 completion of the wagon road to Glacier Point allowed guests to visit the Mountain House in relative comfort.

More facilities were added to the Mountain House as the years progressed.

Here is a lovely view of Half Dome, taken from the covered porch at the Mountain House.

Oakdale rancher and guide Emmett Preston takes a break on the porch of the Mountain House. Many Mariposa-area ranchers worked as summer packers and guides in Yosemite. (Courtesy of the Preston/Fiske family.)

Emmett Preston conducts his charges before leaving the Mountain House for the Four Mile Trail back to Yosemite Valley. (Courtesy of the Preston/Fiske family.)

By 1918, the Glacier Point Hotel, built by the Desmond Company and the San Francisco construction firm of Gutleben Brothers, was complete. The hotel was not an immediate success; high room rates kept visitors from staying more than one night and most preferred to stay in Yosemite Valley.

Positioned to have great views of Half Dome and the high Sierra, the Glacier Point Hotel slowly gained favor but still did poorly as a business.

The cost of building the Glacier Point Hotel, and the attempt to build the Grizzly Hotel in the valley, proved too much of a financial strain for Desmond. With the consolidation of the Curry Company and the Yosemite Park Company in 1924, Curry took over the operation of the hotel. (Photograph by Ralph H. Anderson.)

In this photograph of the sitting porch at the Glacier Point Hotel, the older Mountain House can be seen in the background. The Mountain House eventually became hotel employee housing. Altogether, 90 rooms were available in the two units.

This photograph shows the west side of the Glacier Point Hotel with the main entrance visible.

This is the dining room of the Glacier Point Hotel, with the fireplace in the center. The dual hearth faced both the dining room and the main lounge beyond.

Here is a stunning view of Vernal and Nevada Falls, taken from the porch of the Glacier Point Hotel.

Here is Glacier Point Hotel, seen from the west under a blanket of deep snow. The light construction of the hotel required maintenance personnel to live in the building during the winter. Their main job was to keep the snow off the roof so it would not collapse.

One of the main attractions in Yosemite Valley's early days was the Yosemite Firefall. Wood was gathered at Glacier Point, burned to charcoal, and slowly pushed over the point to entertain the crowds below with a cascade of sparks. Begun by James McCauley about 1872, the event was only an occasional one. When David Curry opened Camp Curry in 1899, he reinvented the Firefall, and it continued on and off until 1969, when it was discontinued by the Park Service.

CAMP CURRY'S FIRE FALL.

In this photograph, coals from a campfire are pushed over Glacier Point during Firefall.

Yosemite woodcutter Bill Bomprezzi, pictured here with his 1936 Mack Truck, stands on Glacier Point with Half Dome in the background. (Courtesy of Bill Bomprezzi.)

Bomprezzi would gather the red fir bark and stack it at Glacier Point before the Firefall. Larry is the young helper. (Courtesy of Bill Bomprezzi.)

Stacks of red fir bark stand ready for the Yosemite Firefall atop Glacier Point. (Courtesy of Bill Bomprezzi.)

Yosemite's first ski run was located at Badger Pass on Glacier Point Road. This area, called Summit Meadow, was soon replaced by a new ski run further east. The ski program was started in the 1930s to encourage year-round use of the park.

In 1935, Badger Pass Lodge was the first structure built by Yosemite Park and Curry Company at the resort. It was damaged by fire in the 1950s and rebuilt as the facility that exists today.

A small track vehicle called a "weasel" was used at Badger Pass for many purposes related to ski-area maintenance. The author once drove a weasel, packing down a ski track by pulling a large cylinder.

In the 1940s, this is the operations crew at Badger Pass. In the middle back is Sid Ledson, with his wife, Helen, in front. He managed the crew that operated the lifts and kept the snow shoveled. Pictured here, from left to right, are (first row) Hilmar Torgerson and Bill Bomprezzi; (second row) Ed Waldron, at far left. (Courtesy of the Sid Ledson estate.)

Pictured here is a Snow Cat, used to drag sleds to Glacier Point, as well as for other adventures. (Courtesy of the Sid Ledson estate.)

Here, second from the left, is Nic Fiore, the head of the ski school and summer High Sierra Camps. For more than 40 years, he was a fixture in Yosemite. On the far right is Nic's great friend Leroy "Rusty" Rust, Yosemite postmaster and innovator of many skiing and ice-skating programs. He was raised in the park, as the son of a horse stage driver.

Five

YOSEMITE NORTH, TIOGA ROAD, AND HETCH HETCHY

North of Yosemite Valley is a vast area that has seen little development. The main imprint of man comes from the roads to the northwest and east, which lead to the main destination, Yosemite Valley and on to the San Joaquin Valley.

A series of High Sierra Camps are scattered north and south of Highway 120 (Tioga Road), started by the Desmond Company about 1918. Except for Tuolumne Meadows, all camps today are reached by trail. Facilities are primitive by today's standards but when first proposed, they were upscale.

The establishment of the High Sierra Camps was made possible by the 1915 purchase of the Tioga Road from the Great Sierra Mining Company by Stephen Mather. He in turn gave the road to the U.S. government. Almost immediately, automobiles begin traversing the Sierra over dramatic and scenic Tioga Pass to Lee Vining on the eastern side.

On the western edge of the park, the Tuolumne River drains the highest part of the Yosemite backcountry into the valley known as Hetch Hetchy. In 1919, the City of San Francisco built a dam, creating one of the finest bodies of clean water in the world. Constructed to supply San Francisco with sufficient water for both drinking and firefighting, the project was built in response to a series of disasters that culminated in the 1906 earthquake and fire. Controversy followed the project until 1913, when the U.S. Congress authorized construction by passing the Raker Act after the major opponent, John Muir, had died.

The first dam began construction in 1919, and a railroad was built to move men, materials, and mail to the site. In August 1934, new construction raised the original dam by 85 feet, significantly increasing the storage capacity of the reservoir. Today the Restore Hetch Hetchy Committee is striving to remove the dam, replacing the storage at newer, larger reservoirs downstream. A major issue will be the replacement of the hydroelectric capacity that the system generates. Studies show that there are alternatives to the existing project, but the costs are high. The proposed project has other reservoirs in the vicinity that will not be disturbed.

In this photograph taken from the north rim of Yosemite Valley, a horse and rider take in the view of Half Dome and Clouds Rest.

John Muir spent a good deal of his life bringing protection to the Sierra. His interest in the backcountry is evidenced by his many trips above the tree line and the founding of the Muir Trail, a 211-mile-long trail that connects with the Pacific Crest Trail from the north. Unfortunately, Muir's influence failed to stop the Hetch Hetchy dam project.

Chinese Camp is a mining town in the foothills of the Sierras, west of the park. It is here that the railroad from the San Joaquin valley met the stages, which would take the Big Oak Flat Road to Yosemite Valley. Photographer A. C. Beck chronicled the early activity at his gallery in Chinese Camp. (Courtesy of Howard Egling.)

Louis Egling, a 22-year-old blacksmith and wheelwright, arrived in Chinese Camp from Germany. He set up a blacksmith shop and instantly became busy building wagons, stages, and freighters, as well as shoeing horses. (Courtesy of Howard Egling.)

By 1876, with the opening of Big Oak Flat Road, Egling's wagon factory was in full production. Examples of his vehicles may be seen today in the collection at the Pioneer History Center in Wawona. (Courtesy of Howard Egling.)

Businesses such as the Chinese Camp, Livery, Feed, and Sale (horse and mule rentals) used Egling's wagons to deliver to the ranches as well as within Yosemite. (Photograph by A. C. Beck.)

Egling's most famous stages carried large groups of visitors to Yosemite. The Big Oak Flat Road ended on the tallest slopes on the north side of Yosemite Valley. (Photograph by A. C. Beck.)

Pictured here is part of the development at Crocker's Station, with the mining ditch and mill in background. (Photograph by A. C. Beck.)

Photographer Beck photographed life throughout Yosemite. Here is his photograph of the tunnel tree in Tuolumne Grove at the edge of Crane Flat. This attraction was part of Big Oak Flat Road. (Photograph by A. C. Beck.)

The children in this cart were all members of one family near Chinese Camp. (Photograph by A. C. Beck.)

Here are some of Egling's stages on Big Oak Flat Road in wintertime. (Photograph by A. C. Beck.)

A. C. Beck's gallery in Chinese Camp became a gathering point for locals to enjoy Mrs. Beck's gardens. Water was not plentiful when Chinese laborers, who were denied claims on the nearby Tuolumne River, started the town. Instead, they would "dry sluice" their diggings to separate the gold. (Photograph by A. C. Beck.)

Pictured here is Cow Camp at Ackerson Meadows, originally known as Buckley Meadows. The property, purchased from forty-niner James T. Ackerson by T. C. Carlon, became the base of his summer cattle operation. (Photograph by A. C. Beck.)

Cattle pioneer Tim C. Carlon was photographed in Hetch Hetchy with young cowboy Roy Earl Cadrett. (Courtesy of John Cadrett.)

Pictured here is the late, great Hetch Hetchy Valley on the Tuolumne River. Cattleman Tim Carlon leased this pasture from the Park Service. His use of the valley, as well as that of other cattlemen, ended with the building of O'Shaughnessy Dam, that created Hetch Hetchy Reservoir and is now used as the main water supply for San Francisco.

The floor of Hetch Hetchy Valley is lower than Yosemite, and there is quite a bit of differing vegetation. However, it was formed by the same glacier scouring and erosion as Yosemite Valley, and similar rock faces and waterfalls caused Muir to declare that this valley was Yosemite's twin.

In this view from the valley floor, Hetch Hetchy's grassy meadow is visible, along with the black oaks that the Native Americans favored for acorns and a mixed conifer forest.

This view looks west downstream towards the dam site of the Hetch Hetchy Valley.

The O'Shaughnessy Dam was finished in 1923 and was designed to accommodate an increase in height. Later an 85-foot increase in the dam summit boosted storage capacity by 75 percent. This was done to allow the year-round operation of the Moccasin Power House (located below Big Oak Flat).

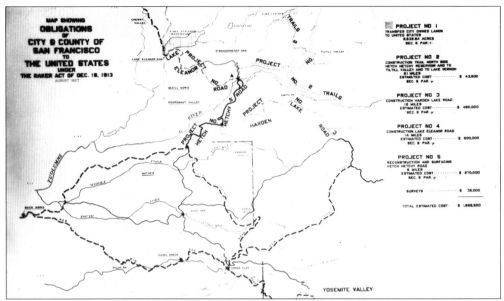

This map shows the extent of the Hetch Hetchy project and the trails and roads that the City and County of San Francisco were obligated to construct as the result of the 1913 Raker Act.

The nearly completed dam and its growing impoundment are pictured here. The book *Hetch Hetchy and its Railroad* by Ted Wurm gives the complete history of the construction of O'Shaughnessy Dam and the railroad that was an important part of the project.

Tioga Road, originally called the Great Sierra Wagon Road, was constructed in 1883 to serve the Tioga Mine. The mine could be reached from the east side of the Sierras but needed a more direct route to the west. The mine failed in 1884, barely a year after the road was constructed.

One of the remarkable landmarks along the route of Tioga Road is Tenaya Lake, still frozen here

in the spring, *c.* 1970. (Photograph by author.)

In 1915, Stephen Mather and a group of friends purchased Tioga Road and donated the new acquisition to the federal government. Almost immediately, the road was available for use through the park and connected with the new state road to the east.

By 1918, the Desmond Company began constructing the High Sierra Camps, starting with this one along Tioga Road at Tenaya Lake. Myrtle Schlageter McSwain of Mariposa was the camp's 18-year-old manager; she came from Chicago for the experience.

uolumne lodge

Another High Sierra Camp was located at Tuolumne Meadows. These mid-summer camps were located about a day's hike apart. Visitors would make the tour carrying essentials and have a dining room to eat in and a real bed to sleep in at the end of each day. These camps still operate today.

This wooden horse bridge carried visitors across the Tuolumne River on their way to and from Glen Aulin.

The Merced Lake High Sierra Camp was a major development for a horse camp. It had a large dining room and served hikers and horse riders along the main Merced River. From this camp, it was a day's hike to the top of Nevada Falls and into Yosemite Valley.

Eadweard Muybridge photographed this stereo pair of horsemen crossing the Tuolumne River in the meadow. Stereo pairs were a popular type of photograph for tourists, as they were small and could work in a device that gave a three-dimensional photograph. (Photograph by Eadweard Muybridge.)

A trip from Bodie to Yosemite might start off in the old mining town in a bus provided by the Yosemite Transportation System.

Traveling west among the blooming desert flowers became a lovely preamble to the sharp ascent of the eastern side of the Sierras, as seen in this 1918 photograph. There were no services as there are today.

Located on the western edge of Mono Lake, the Tioga Lodge was a popular stopping point for hikers before climbing the Sierras.

Leaving the high desert, one could look back to see Mono Lake in the distance.

Many rock slides have closed Tioga Road over the years. This turn is about three quarters of the way to Ellery Lake.

Passing along the talus slopes of the climb out of Lee Vining Canyon, one can appreciate the impressive efforts of the road's builders.

Almost at the top near Ellery Lake, rock and steel bridges connect the slide areas. Many times in the past, this road has been destroyed completely. Today when driving near this area, observers can see the old road above the highway.

This photograph shows an early automobile leaving Yosemite National Park at the 9,941-foot-high Tioga Pass, one of the highest passes in the Sierras. Seventy-three miles from Yosemite Lodge in the valley, the area offers a wonderful selection of woods, meadows, lakes, and granite peaks. It is also the gateway to the east side of Yosemite, with Lee Vining, Mono Lake, and Bodie all within a short distance. Fairly soon after the pass, the vegetation and geology changes to high desert species. Silver mining characterized this area early on, as many miners, weary of struggling in the Mariposa area, left for the east side seeking a new future. Towns sprang up along what is now State Highway 395. Lee Vining was one of those miners from the Mariposa region who crossed the Sierras, marveling at the sharp descent to the desert floor and searching for gold all along the way. The town of Lee Vining is named for him.

To the west of Sawmill Flat Campground, on a reasonably easy trail, one can find the remains of Bennettville, pictured here when still active. A couple of the buildings, preserved by the cold of 10,000 feet, are still standing.

As pictured here, Tioga Road follows the Dana Fork of the Tuolumne River inside the park.

Mono Lake, at the end of Tioga Pass Road and near the town of Lee Vining, is a primordial lake that has high concentrations of mineral. The mineralization causes the formation of tufa towers, which are the accumulation of salts and the secretions of tiny life forms of calcareous algae. Because of evaporation, this landlocked lake, although fed by Sierra streams, has become more briny than the ocean. It will only support various species of shrimp, crustaceans, and plankton but provides food for a myriad of birds that feed and reproduce here. (Photograph by author.)

Six

BODIE

In the summer of 1859, William Bodey prospected north and east of Mono Lake, finding a promising placer of gold on the site of the town of Bodie. That winter, Bill Bodey died, but the placer location would continue and carry his name. The location proved so rich that in the period of 1879 through 1881, the population of the town was estimated to be between 10,000 and 13,000. This location was around 9,000 feet, however, and temperatures could drop to 40 degrees below Fahrenheit, with snow as much as 20 feet deep. Since the mining was underground, however, work could go on year-round.

It is said that during its peak period, the town averaged six murders a week, gaining the reputation as the "Wildest Town in the West." Fire and disease were the town's greatest enemies. Smallpox and other diseases would run wild in the population; the cemetery is crowded with children and young people who succumbed to the harshness of life.

In the late 1960s, the author began a photographic record of the town of Bodie. Many of the photographs reflect the town before it became a state park, rather than the stabilized version that exists today. Visitors to Bodie should be prepared for a slow trip but one that is certainly worthwhile. There are virtually no other early mining camps that still show as wide a variety of buildings and artifacts. Many structures here were lost in a series of fires, and the remaining houses and the stores still contain contents when they were abandoned during those events, frozen in time.

Bodie has a direct connection with the Mother Lode region of Mariposa County and Yosemite. Being on the eastern side of the Sierras, not far from the park boundary and easily accessible on a day trip, this mining town is a fine example of 19th-century pioneer life. Unspoiled like other mining towns, it is easy to appreciate the difficulty of living at such an elevation, remote from civilization and yet self-contained with a school, church, stores, and rooming houses. The striking color of the wood in the town, mostly made of eastern slope Ponderosa pine, is still a rich reddish brown. One would expect much more deterioration than has happened in Bodie, but the high altitude here acts as a preservative through the years.

From Bodie's main street, one can see the principal mine that supported the town. The building on the right was the Bodie Hotel.

Bricks were used in some construction in an attempt to create fireproof buildings. The middle building seen here was the International Order of Odd Fellows (IOOF) Hall; the building on the right was Miners Hall.

Bodie's general store, complete with gas pumps, is pictured here. The contents of the store gives one an idea of the range of merchandise available many years ago.

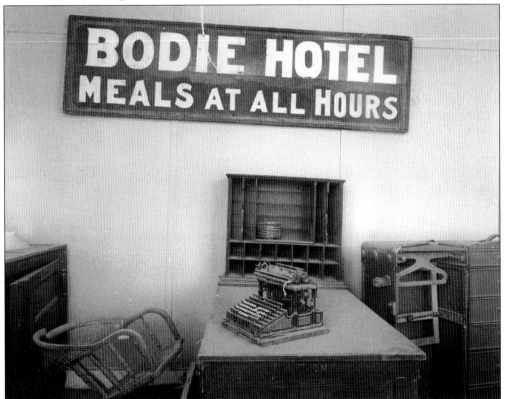

The sign in the office of the Bodie Hotel indicates that this was once a 24-hour town.

The Miners Hall is now used as a museum. Note the lightbulb above the door; electricity came to Bodie from a generator at Lundy Lake. It ran the mills and lighted the businesses and homes.

This bottle collection, pictured in front of a Bodie residence in 1973, is no longer here. Preservationists feared the fragile shelving would collapse.

Here is the window of the La Belle Beauty Shop in 1973.

This photograph shows Bodie's barbershop and store, isolated from the rest of the town because of fire.

Pictured here is the pool hall, once a popular spot in the Bodie Hotel.

Here are the interior contents of the Bodie Store.

The interior of this miner's house shows the walls and ceilings covered by wallpaper attached to cloth. This common construction method often contributed to the rapid destruction of buildings by fire.

Bodie was a wide-open place in more ways than one—a fact to which this saloon and its gambling tables attest.

Pictured here is the Bodie Mine Mill.

This photograph depicts the stately Bodie church, complete with a storage shed.

Here is a row of some of the better homes of Bodie.

This Bodie room has a baby crib and dresser. Scattered items still in the dressing stand suggest a quick departure took place here.

Here is the front of the Bodie Store; note the dressmaker's dummy in the window.

This residence held the bottle collection pictured on page 120, which has now been removed. Care and time was taken during construction to afford elegant design features such as the glassed-in shelving.

Sadly, the Bodie mortuary was a busy place. Many children's caskets are still on display here.

The wooden sidewalks of Bodie's main street are pictured here by Miners Hall.

Across America, People are Discovering Something Wonderful. Their Heritage.

Arcadia Publishing is the leading local history publisher in the United States. With more than 3,000 titles in print and hundreds of new titles released every year, Arcadia has extensive specialized experience chronicling the history of communities and celebrating America's hidden stories, bringing to life the people, places, and events from the past. To discover the history of other communities across the nation, please visit:

www.arcadiapublishing.com

Customized search tools allow you to find regional history books about the town where you grew up, the cities where your friends and family live, the town where your parents met, or even that retirement spot you've been dreaming about.